The Black Flag Manual
By Captain Blue Eye

www.PiratesBuriedTreasures.com

The Black Flag Manual

ISBN 978-0-578-03587-1

Copyright © 2009
Captain Blue Eye
All Rights Reserved.

www.PiratesBuriedTreasures.com

The Black Flag Manual
By Captain Blue Eye

This paperback version of The Black Flag Manual is not to be considered a complete copy of the leather-bound version produced by Captain Blue Eye.

Pirates seeking the complete leather-bound version of The Black Flag Manual should visit:

www.PiratesBuriedTreasures.com

Paperback versions of The Black Flag Manual are handbooks, which may be used as a quick reference while engaged in treasure hunting and exploration. Pirates are urged to plunder and review the leather-bound version of The Black Flag Manual in its entirety when conditions are appropriate for deep concentration & thought.

The Black Flag Manual

Table Of Contents

I. Welcome Aboard

II. Chain-O-Command

III. Leadership & Discipline
    1. Leadership
    2. Discipline
    3. Reputation
    4. Respect
    5. The Captain's Articles

IV. Seamanship & Navigation
    1. Line & Rope
    2. The Ten Line Orders
    3. Splicing A Line
    4. Knots, Bends & Hitches
    5. Piloting
    6. Dead Reckoning (DR)
    7. Magnetic Compass
    8. Tides & Currents

V. The Seven Elements Of Captain Blue Eye
    1. Eternal Optimism
    2. Benevolent Compassion
    3. Profound Perception
    4. Enduring Charisma
    5. Marksman At Arms
    6. Cavalier By Cutlass
    7. Invincibility At Sea

VI. The Captain's Treasures
     1. Types Of Treasures
     2. Treasure Coins

VII. The Captain's Caches

VIII. The Captain's Landmarks

IX. The Captain's Scuttlebutt

X. Economy
     1. Trade Goods
     2. Commodities
     3. Pirate Notes

XI. Items Of Interest
     1. Artifacts & Idols
     2. Buried Treasure Bottles
     3. Captain's Cards
     4. Scrolls
     5. Ships Logs
     6. Tavern Journals
     7. Treasure Maps

XII. Online Adventures
     1. Pirate Profiles
     2. Personal Effects
     3. Pirate Challenges
     4. Online Locations

XIII. Glossary

From The Captain

When The Black Flag Manual first appeared in the hands of pirates, there were few sources of information to guide Wogs through the trials and tribulations of life at sea. The Black Flag Manual became the first official publication and written source to provide practical information to landlubbers and sailors with a desire to become successful pirates.

Life at sea is among the most challenging trades to experience and one of the most respected occupations to adopt as a career for those in search of adventure. Raising sail and heading for the horizon is not the only requirement for experiencing adventures at sea. For those lacking knowledge, experience and/or leadership, there be foul reefs ahead and a burial at sea. Properly preparing for the challenges ahead is the fundamental basis for a successful career as a pirate. The Black Flag Manual is the beginning.

This unique & highly prized manual is the product of considerable time and effort by the famed, all-be-it notorious Captain Blue Eye. Many windless days and star filled nights went into the development of this priceless manual.

A number of loyal crewmembers are to be commended for their efforts in providing loyal service to the Captain. The Captain's unwavering ability to provide words of passage during battle was equally matched by Patch's steadfast devotion to make written records while under siege.

Stumpy's artistic ability to enhance the pages within with residual powder & shot gives the manual an essence of art with a flavor of war.

Pontos is to be commended for his craftsmanship in creating each leather-bound cover to ensure long lasting durability during high seas adventures.

The Black Flag Manual will give you a broad understanding of your expectations while serving as a member of Captain Blue Eye's Crew. This manual is sacred and shall be carried in your satchel and within swords reach in time of need. The Black Flag Manual will assist you in becoming an essential part of this notorious & successful brotherhood of pirates.

It will be an integral part of your daily life and become a cherished possession long after your service. Keep it close at hand and allow no crown or authority to ever retain possession from you.

In addition, allow no authority to deprive you of your right for a euphoric life full of adventures.

Fair Winds & Following Seas,

The Captain

Captain Blue Eye

Ahoy Matey & Welcome Aboard

Welcome Aboard The Sterne's Revenge! These words are rarely used and carry significant meaning to sailors and landlubbers seeking a successful career as a pirate. To hear these words, you must have encountered one of the most profound decisions a sailor can make.

Volunteering to come aboard as a member of Captain Blue Eye's Crew, you have made a decision that will carry through your bloodline for generations to come. As a member of the most successful pirate crew to sail the seven seas, you have accepted a new and challenging course in life that will no doubt take you to new lands, new adventures and a rewarding life full of experiences and treasures to last a lifetime.

Captain Blue Eye's crew is a unique organization designed to be efficient and effective in all means and manner. Simplistic in essence, yet complex in nature, Captain Blue Eye's Crew will become your family of families. More protective than your father and more nurturing than your mother, the brotherhood will propagate camaraderie far beyond your highest expectations.

Your desire to become a pirate no-doubt began as a young child with dreams of adventures and treasures. The life of a farmer or blacksmith surely lacked the entertainment value you sought, not to mention the luxurious lifestyle preferred by those among the living. Passing stories of rich soils and bumper crops does not quite demand the respect and admiration from younger generations. What is a rusty sword of the past without the history of bloodshed? Seeking a new path in life, you stake your claim in history and cast your faith beyond the horizon.

As many a member may share, most family bonds are cast to the shores upon acceptance into the life of a pirate. Families may refute your intent and desire to become a pirate and some may seek assistance from the crown to change your mind.

In time, whether inspired by admiration of adventures or respect for familial ties, many a family will no doubt recant their beliefs for your occupation once they reap the benefits bestowed upon them.

To ease your transition into the life of a pirate, you must first become familiar with certain terminology, customs and traditions among life at sea. Pirates use many different words for the same things you had at home. This may be deemed as tradition, code or both, but a thorough understanding of each words meaning is paramount in having a smooth transition to living a pirate's life aboard The Sterne's Revenge.

A few terms you must immediately become versed in are relatively simple. Beds are bunks and bathrooms are heads. Floors are decks and walls are bulkheads. Stairways are ladders and drinking fountains are scuttlebutts. Scuttlebutt is also known as "the latest rumors".

For a detailed list of the common terms and phrases used onboard, review the glossary in the aft section of this manual. Understanding the terms and phrases used aboard will enhance your ability to master all skills and reduce your training time required to achieve qualification as a full share member of The Captain's Crew. While aboard ship, we are a crew. We work together, eat together, fight together & sleep together. Nothing shall come between The Captain and his crew nor shall there be hostilities without a common foe.

Chain-O-Command

Understanding & abiding by the Chain-O-Command while aboard The Sterne's Revenge is essential in all conditions and environments. Those not willing to give respect to or follow the orders of senior officers will be punished in accordance with the code established in this manual.

All hands shall abide by The Captain's Code and shall give due respect to the ranks and positions above, as well as below that which is currently held. The ranks within The Captain's Crew are as follows:

Officer Ranks	Enlisted Ranks
First Mate	Lanyard Grabber
Navigator	Powder Monkey
Quartermaster	Deck Hand
Boatswain	Deck Swabber
Gunner	Scallywag
Helmsman	Scurvy Dog
Boatswains Mate	Chum Master
Sailmaker	Barnacle Bait
Foc'sle Keeper	Plankton
GallyMaid	Wog

A landlubber may start his or her career as a simple Wog, but The Captain provides each crewmember with the opportunities necessary to advance your career as a pirate. Education in all respects of seamanship & navigation may be required in order to qualify for a high-ranking officers position, but only the truly devoted & loyal crew members choose to stay onboard for a long lasting career.

Remember that each and every crewmember started out at the bottom and every senior officer was once a Wog. The Captain gives no favor to heritage or lineage and only promotes efficient and effective performance.

Pirates come and go and there will always be a hull full of eager landlubbers willing to trade their farming shovels for The Captain's lines. Many pirates are simply content with filling their own chests with The Captain's treasures. For those seeking adventures & treasures, then a pirate's life may be for you! For those willing to put forth the effort required and serve The Captain as a loyal member of his crew, then a lucrative career you shall have!

Leadership & Discipline

Leadership

Captain Blue Eye consistently reminds his crew.....

"Before you can lead, you must have followers. Before you can be an effective leader, you must have willing followers." The Captain expects each and every crewmember to be a loyal follower under The Black Flag, whether in The Captain's presence or away. Even those not currently aboard the Sterne's Revenge, but still sworn to the Captain's Code are expected to maintain their loyalty to The Captain & the brotherhood.

As a loyal follower to Captain Blue Eye, you are expected to learn and understand the qualities of leadership, discipline, standards of conduct and seamanship, as well as master at least one specific skill. All members of Captain Blue Eye's crew train on the various duties assigned aboard ship, but are required to master at least one skill. Having mastered at least one skill is a requirement of becoming a line officer under The Captain.

Captain Blue Eye is so concerned with "Quality of Leadership", he has been known to attack an opposing vessel with a well-known terror at the helm, only to remove the captain, address the crew and let the crew appoint a new captain. To some sailors, leadership is simply getting a job done. According to Captain Blue Eye, leadership is "how a job gets done".

If a captain gets a job done, but loses the respect of his crew in the process, he is not a good leader and does not deserve to be at the helm of even the smallest canoe. Any captain of any size vessel, with efforts resulting in dissention, disorganization, ineffectiveness and/or poor morale will eventually lead to mutiny.

A captain who alienates his men will only hurt his crew, as well as himself in the long run. If you alienate the men you will eventually need to count on, especially during combat, then those men will not be there when you need them.

Leadership is the art of influencing people to win their obedience, confidence, respect and willingness to cooperate. You may be given authority to lead, but to be an effective and lasting leader, you must first earn the respect of your crew.

No crew shall withstand a barrage of chain-shot for a leader they do not respect, but they will hold steady for a broadside opportunity if they respect the gentleman at the helm.

Discipline

Under the Black Flag with Captain Blue Eye, the term punishment has evolved into what is known as discipline. Punishment, by definition, is a penalty inflicted for an offense or fault. Captain Blue Eye sees little to no benefit for punishment and has adopted guidelines for a more reasonable and effective measure known as discipline. Discipline involves the act of training an individual to act in accordance with rule or regulations.

The training is designed to develop or improve a specific skill, which will ultimately bring desired results. The Captain believes that if you fail to provide training to develop or modify a certain behavior, then you are bound to experience the same or similar unfavorable results. With training, an individual may adopt or change their behavior to provide more favorable results. The results of discipline over punishment are much more favorable as with the difference between asking a crewmember to complete a task and telling the crewmember to complete the task.

Asking provides a more positive environment and gives the crewmember a sense of control. Telling removes any possible sense of control for the crewmember and may eventually lead to poor morale, dissention and mutiny.

Reputation

Captain Blue Eye has a notorious reputation of being a fierce and cruel Captain, but this reputation did not evolve from a member of the crew or even the Captain himself. This reputation evolved from the many stories told by landlubbers who failed to understand how and why a sailor would remain onboard for many long adventures without ever seeing their family members back home.

Truth be known, Captain Blue Eye is a fair and just Captain who does not exactly "lead" his crew. Captain Blue Eye "inspires" his crew to follow him and achieve the impossible. Whether is be the onslaught of the royal navy or the jaws of a hurricane, The Captain inspires his crew to go against the odds and accomplish what is generally considered impossible.

The Captain is confident in the training of his crew and the execution of their abilities. He knows their limits better than they know their own name and exploits their strengths while avoiding their weaknesses.

Respect

As a loyal member of Captain Blue Eye's Crew, you must also earn the respect of your fellow crewmembers. Crowed on board a treasure galleon for many days, weeks or even months at a time, personalities may spark and tempers may flare.

While at sea, crewmembers must get along and get along well. There are no pubs, taverns or inns to escape to and the size of a large galleon may seem like a small skiff after only a few days at sea. Privacy is rare and personal space is limited while underway so respect be of the utmost importance for all members on board.

Attitudes toward other crewmembers must be handled with care and there are certain qualities and characteristics a crewmember must possess or acquire to endure harsh conditions at sea. To insure peace and camaraderie among crewmembers, each member must have and maintain a high level of consideration, respect and tolerance for all other members onboard. While at sea or in combat situations, each crewmember relies on all other crewmembers to do their job well.

A crewmember efficient and effective in their duties and responsibilities is a valuable member to have as part of Captain Blue Eye's crew. A crewmember lacking efficiency or effectiveness may become a fundamental weakness of the operational capabilities of the warship. Only those willing to do their fair share shall have a plank with The Captain's crew.

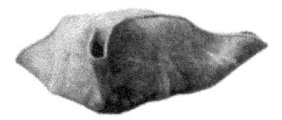

The Captain's Articles

I. The Captain's Word is the governing authority at sea, as well as land. All crewmembers shall convey the utmost respect to the captain, to his ship and to his mates and no member may oppose The Captain's word or desire.

II. Every crewmember shall have equal title to fresh provisions.

III. Every crewmember shall have equal title to grog and rum when released from holds.

IV. Every crewmember shall be called fairly in turn by list for prize upon drop of anchor in port.

V. Upon crossing brow, every crewmember surrenders goods to the Quartermaster for log & holds. (removes temptation to steal from other shipmates).

VI. All lights and candles are to be put out at eight o'clock at night: if any of the crew, after that hour still remained inclined for leisure, they are to do it on the open deck.

VII. All crewmembers shall keep their piece, pistols, and cutlass clean and fit for service.

VIII. No stow-aways onboard.

IX. No Dissension among the crew.

X. No crewmember shall take game or rest during combat.

XI. Desertion of ship or quarters in battle is punishable by death or marooning.

XII. The bravest of crew, as voted among peers, during time of battle shall be given first plunder of a single item.

XIII. Every soul coming aboard as crew shall accept & sign The Captain's Articles prior to crossing the brow.

Leadership & Discipline Provides Direction To A Successful Adventure!

- Captain Blue Eye

Seamanship & Navigation

As with any enterprise created through the cohesive bond of multiple independent tasks working simultaneously together, the process of sailing large ships beyond the horizon requires a network of well-trained individuals working together to achieve a common goal. While some positions on a vessel may be quite different from other position just steps away, each position on the vessel shares one common goal. To maintain operational capabilities of the ship, thus enabling The Captain & crew to continue adventures beyond the horizon.

The most landlocked Wog capable of crossing the brow of a ship may be able to raise anchor & sail beyond the horizon. Leaving the safe haven of your homeport is the easiest part of any adventure. The real challenge is being able to endure the elements of each adventure, yet somehow manage to return to port with hull and dignity intact.

Many an unprepared sailor and ship have ventured beyond the horizon only to find a watery grave. The main difference between a round trip and a one-way adventure lies in the training of the crew. Crewmembers fulfilling their duties as required ensure the continued success of the adventure ahead.

Unlike most captains to sail the seven seas, Captain Blue Eye firmly believes in training all crewmembers in the art of seamanship & navigation. Since the first sails were raised on the earliest of sea going vessels, men learned various skills to assist them in fulfilling their duties aboard ship. Mastering these skills meant the difference between a one-way journey and a round trip adventure.

With all the hazards associated with life at sea, Captain Blue Eye understands the odds of a successful adventure are greatly increased with a well-trained crew. The Captain also takes his beliefs to another level and insisted on cross-training each crewmember to enable the crew as a whole to continue an adventure or battle, even with an unexpected donation to Davy Jones Locker.

Having each member of the crew trained in various skills & positions aboard ship has proven to be an invaluable asset during many adventures. The flexibility associated with cross training provides many opportunities for individuals as well as the crew as a whole, which are not otherwise possible if a position is dependant on a single qualified shipmate. Cross training has enabled crewmembers to "cover one another" while underway, thereby providing opportunities for entertainment and rest below deck without compromising ships operations.

The additional periods of rest and relaxation while underway ensures The Captain's crew is always capable of sustaining extended operations while at General Quarters. Local tavern scuttlebutt even provides word of an unusual practice of resting a percentage of the crew while engaged in battle. This practice ensures there be fresh hands available in time of need. This practice has been deemed as "highly unlikely" and renounced by all other captains of the sea, but it would begin to explain how Captain Blue Eye can sustain superior operations at sea while engaged in battle with multiple warships.

This ability of The Captain's crew to continue operations and engage in battle even though severe damage is quite apparent eventually spawned one of the seven elements of The Captain's reputation.

This element is known as "Invincibility At Sea".

As an able bodied seaman serving Captain Blue Eye, you must be able to perform various tasks which require extensive use of line. The art of handling and working with line & rope is known as Marlinespike Seamanship. The name is derived from the tool used in working with line & rope.

Line & Rope

The standard line in use aboard most sea going vessels is the three-strand line. In three-strand line, the fibers are twisted into yarns or threads. The yarns are then twisted in the opposite direction into strands and the strands are twisted back in the first direction, into ropes.

Rope can have either three or four strands and the direction the strands are twisted determines the lay of the rope. If the strands are twisted to the left, the rope is said to be "left laid". If the strands are twisted to the right, the rope is said to be "right laid".

Braided lines have advantages over twisted ropes. They will not kink or cockle and they will not flex open, which tends to allow for dirt and other foreign objects to contaminate the line.

One disadvantage of some braided lines is their design makes it impossible for a sailor to inspect the inner threads for possible damage. Some of the types of braids you will be required to master are known as double braids, hollow braids, solid braids & stuffer braids.

Properly stowing coils of line is mandatory onboard The Captain's ship. Many a crew faced the depths of Davy's Locker due in part to a lack of preparation and organization. While conducting operations at sea, especially when engaged in combat, a crew is more efficient & effective when lacking obstructions such as loose or tangle line.

A clear deck allows for a smooth transition from broadside to broadside and proper footing is essential if the use of sword & sabre is due.

Coils of line shall be stowed in the boatswain's locker when not in use. Clear of the deck and on shelves or racks. Coils of line shall never be covered as to prevent access or evaporation of moisture. When stowed in locker, coils shall be arranged in order of size and positioned as to allow immediate access to the ends of line. Except during fire & cannonade, all lines deemed wet shall be dried topside before stowed within lockers. This measure prevents mildew and rot.

When using rope & line, all hands shall follows The Captain's Line Orders. The Ten Line Orders are as follows:

1. Inspect line before use.
2. Never use damaged line.
3. Coil right-laid line right-handed (clockwise).
4. Line shall not contact stays, guys or other standing rigging.
5. When surging around bitts & capstands, surge line smoothly.
6. If line is chafed or damaged, cut & splice before use.
7. Whip all line ends.
8. Do not drag line over rough objects.
9. Keep bitts, chocks & cleats in smooth condition.
10. Apply loads slowly & carefully.

Knots, Bends & Hitches

Along with splicing line, the use of knots & bends are particularly useful in life about ship. A knot is a technique in which the line is usually bent to itself. The knot may be used to form an eye or a knob or it may be used to secure a cord or line around an object. A bend, on the other hand, is primarily used to join two lines together.

There are four classes of knots of which a crewmember must master in order to become a full share deckhand.

1. Knots at the end of a line, which are used to fasten upon itself or around an object.

2. Knots for bending two lines together.

3. Knots, which are used to secure a line to a ring or spar.

4. Knots, which are used to give finish to the end of a line and prevent unreeving.

Reeving Line Bend: This is the best knot used when it is necessary to bend two lines together that must reeve around a capstan or winch drum.

Fisherman's Bend: This knot is used to bend a line to a becket or eye, as a messenger to a mooring line. It may also be used to secure a rope to a buoy or a hawser to the ring of an anchor.

Bowline: This is a temporary eye in the end of a line. A Bowline will not slip or jam and a Bowline on a bight is commonly used to sling a man over the side since it will not slip.

Masthead Knot: These knots are set at the top of masts & stays. Shrouds are secured to these knots.

Spanish Bowline: This is the knot to use when you need two eyes in a line. Many prefer it to the Bowline because the bights are set and will not shift back and forth when weight is applied.

Rolling Hitch: This is the most useful & important hitch to be used on deck. It is used for passing a stopper on a boatfall or mooring line when you are shifting the fall or line from a winch or capstan to cleat or bit. If the Rolling Hitch is properly tied, it will hold as long as there is strain on the hitch.

Timber Hitch: This hitch is used on logs, spars and planks or other objects with rough surfaces.

Marline Hitch: This hitch is used on furled sails, awnings and double-up mooring lines. When clinched, this hitch will hold tight.

Blackwall Hitch: This hitch (single or double) is used to secure a rope to a hook. It can be made rather quickly and if tied properly, is quite secure.

Round turn with two half hitches: This combination is useful when used on a ring, eye or spar. It is preferred when attaching to a spar because it grips and holds it's position.

Barrel Hitch: This hitch is used to hoist most objects, but is most effective in hoisting barrels, drums and boxes without tops.

Square Knot: This knot, also known as a reef knot, is used for bending lines together. This knot is useful for light work, but will jam under heavy tension.

Figure Eight Knot: This knot is used to prevent the end of a line from unreeving through a block or eyebolt.

Catspaw: This is used to secure a sling to a cargo hook. It will not slip or jam.

Carrick Bend: This is used to bend two hawsers together. It will not slip or jam and can be easily untied, even if submerged in water for extended periods of time.

Splicing A Line

The term splicing means to permanently join the ends of two lines or bending one line back on itself to form a permanent loop. When a splice is properly done, the splice will not weaken the line. A proper splice will run over a sheave or other object much easier than any knot. The three types of splicing are known as The Short Splice, The Long Splice and The Eye Splice.

When making a short splice, both ends of a line are laid for a short distance and the strands are interlaced. One strand is tucked through the lay of another, which has been properly opened with a marlinespike, then the other strands are tucked in a similar fashion. Threads are then cut away from the ends of each tucked strand until they are at least two-thirds their original size. The ends are then tucked again. Once again, the ends are cut away until they are one-third their original size. A third and last tuck is taken which produces a clean and proper splice.

A long splice is made with the same technique, but the ends are laid further than a short splice. An Eye Splice is made the same way, but the line is first brought back on itself with enough slack to allow for the desired size of eye. After the strands are tucked into the line to form the eye, the remaining lengths of the strands are tucked into the body of the line.

Piloting

Piloting is a term used to describe a method of determining position and directing the movements of a ship by reference to landmarks, navigation aids or soundings. Piloting is the primary means of navigation when entering and leaving port and is also used when passing through coastal areas. In piloting, the captain obtains warning of danger, fixes the position frequently and accurately determines the proper course of immediate action. Lookouts are extremely useful when piloting coastal or other hazardous areas.

Dead Reckoning (DR)

Dead Reckoning is a method of navigation, primarily used at sea, in which a position is determined by plotting the direction and distance traveled from a known point of departure. A vessel, which is underway, is moving with or against various elements such as wind, wave and ocean currents.

A ship may leave a specific point, steer an exact course according to true bearing between the point of departure and the destination, but still wind up a good distance away from the intended destination depending on how much leeway she makes. Dead reckoning seldom produces exact results and is therefore considered an estimate at best.

Magnetic Compass

The mysteries and stories of the magnetic compass vary from captain to captain and many a sailor lacking the skills necessary to understand the principles have found themselves part of a reef or shoal at journey's end. Those standing the test of time and maintaining their loyalty to Captain Blue Eye shall receive detailed instruction on the usage of a magnetic compass, but are sworn to secrecy regarding the principles and theories.

Many rumors sail about regarding the principles associated with the magnetic compass. Some claim the proper usage is associated with extensive education spanning years of instruction while others lay claim to "karma" or a "Divine Right For Knowledge". For those that truly seek the knowledge required to effectively master the art of navigation with a magnetic compass, they must research an invaluable phrase....

"Can Dead Men Vote Twice"

- Compass
- Deviation
- Magnetic
- Variation
- True

Tides & Currents

Many who have served under Captain Blue Eye lay claim to possible insanity on the captain's part. His brilliant mind has been overshadowed by abstract thought and farfetched conclusions, which may only be derived through extensive consumption of rum & ale. Of his many theories deemed rubbage in the eye's of the crown, his theories on tides rank above them all.

As per Captain Blue Eye, the term "tide" describes the regular rise and fall of the water level along coastal areas or in a port. The Captain claims the gravitational attraction of the moon is the primary cause of tides. He describes the moon as an object that exerts a very considerable amount of "pull" on the seven seas, which pulls the water away from the earth. The Captain claims there is an almost equal amount of water on the opposite side of the earth, regardless of your relative position.

The Captain claims the world is constantly spinning and moving around the sun in the sky. He also claims there is an invisible force, known as "centrifugal force", which is caused by the spinning motion. This invisible force piles the water up where the pull of the moon is weakest.

The Captain states the moon orbits the earth every twenty-four hours and fifty minutes, thus providing two low and two high tides at any place during that period.

The low and high tides are each twelve hours and twenty-five minutes apart. He also claims the sun also has an effect on the tides, but it is so much farther away than the moon that it's pull is not nearly so great.

A tide, which is said to be moving or rising from low water to high water is said to be flooding. A tide which is falling after a high tide, it is said to be ebbing. Although The Captain's claims seem to be derived through extensive consumption of contaminated rum & ale, there appears to be notable signs consistent with those words, which he tends to speak of.

Captain Blue Eye has also discussed the elements of currents, which seem to be quite exact and may appear to validate his claim of the moon affecting the tides. In most harbors and inlets, the tides tend to be the primary causes of currents. However, if the harbor or inlet is situated on a large river, its flow may have a significant effect on tidal currents. The strength and flow of a large river may extend the duration of the ebb current as compared to that of a flood. The speed of the ebb may also be considerably greater than that of a flood.

In harbors or inlets where the current is primarily caused by the rise and fall of the tides, the direction and speed of the current is primarily determined by the geometry of the shoreline and contour of the sea floor below. If there is a long and smooth beach or a straight line of course in the water, the current will tend to flow quickly in the center of the course and more slowly in the shallows on either side.

If sailing through such an area, it's best to sail through the center of course if with the current and near the shallows if against the current. If sailing against the current and in the shallows on either side, lookouts are required for signs of troubled waters. Large rocks and fallen trees are common in the shallows. The lack of knowledge in these principles tends to bring dismay upon hostile crews either fleeing from or in pursuit of Captain Blue Eye.

The Seven Elements
Of Captain Blue Eye

The Legend Of Captain Blue Eye is rather unique compared to those of the many inferior and slightly more popular pirate captains. Most pirate captains were fugitives on the run, either from the crown, the local authorities or the many acquaintances they wronged in the past. They were elusive by nature and would prey upon those unfortunate enough to come into contact with them.

As they ventured through life, they would pillage & plunder their way from one day to the next. Each treasure they plundered and each cache they discovered was used to finance their starving appetites and bad habits. Most were poor souls lost in the world, lacking wisdom, compassion and honor. They would use those around them for immediate gratification and given the chance, they would sell their own mother for a mug of rum.

The many stories of these pirates became popular over the years due in part to their atrocious behaviors. They appeared to be free from the governing laws of the lands and they would do as they please, at least until morning greeted them with a hangman's noose.

Many pirate captains were elected to serve on behalf of their crew and some were replaced if they failed to satisfy the desires of the majority. Captain Blue Eye, however, was a unique Captain whose charisma commanded respect from friends & foe's alike. He lived each day as if it was his last and he stayed true to his moral values & virtues. The Captain's unwavering ability to remain loyal to his values gave birth to what is known as the elements of his character.

Captain Blue Eye, on the other hand, serves to please his inner soul. He is an optimistic man with a unique ability to capture the winds of favor and see the best in every moment of life. Adrift at sea, lacking ration & drink, The Captain spies an opportunity to cross the horizon for a new adventure. Lost in the darkness of a deep cavern underground, The Captain enjoys the whisper of the winds and howl of the caves. He is forever seeking the best in every person, place & opportunity and his blatant disregard for negativity is divine at best.

His compassion is unrivaled by clergy, cleric & monk alike. He lives by a rule known to many but followed by few. "The First Be Shame To Me, The Second Unto You...... Let There Be No Second!"

Even when out of favor, The Captain finds just cause to levy compassion.

His perception is unwavering and keen to those near and far. His ability to determine the outcome of any given situation or scenario is unparalleled by the likes of Nostredamous.

The Captain's Charisma gives a true course to his angelic nature. His charm alone commands authority and tends to beguile friends & foe alike to harness the winds for his innermost desires.

For those incapable of coming within winds ear of the Captain's word and determined to inflict harm, they shall be put down by his superior marksmanship. With his meticulous understanding of mathematics & physics, The Captain has been known to execute seven foes with a volley of four shots!

Those swindled into believing they may cut The Captain down by brawn & blade shall find themselves bewildered and bathe in their own blood. Although indignant to the use of sword & saber, The Captain is well disciplined in the art of beheading by blade.

If the word of a sailor or the will of the crown determines just cause for an engagement against The Captain at sea, their last will and testament had better be signed & sealed. The Captain has mastered the skills of seamanship & navigation and requires the same of his crew. Each member is required to flawlessly execute the duties of every position onboard and the crew is capable of successfully engaging multiple warships with as little as fifteen percent hands at the ready.

These unique elements of Captain Blue Eye have been listed in taverns & pubs and display the true character of The Real Captain Blue Eye. The Captain had not requested these elements be publicized. In fact, the owners of these fine establishments grew tired of the many false claims of unworthy souls swearing to be the likes of the true captain.

Those claiming to be Captain Blue Eye, find themselves tested and proven otherwise. Of course, tis' nature of Captain Blue Eye to dismiss claims of being the admired captain, so anyone actually claiming to be, has already proven otherwise.

The elements of The Captain's character have been listed and are commonly referred to as "The Seven Elements Of Captain Blue Eye". Any captain presumed to be the legendary Captain Blue Eye, could be put to the test, thus revealing their false claim. Having knowledge of this list and the order they fall, tends to prove valuable in itself. Many a treasure quest and access to secret locations require knowledge of this information.

The Seven Elements Of Captain Blue Eye Are As Follows:

1. Eternal Optimism
2. Benevolent Compassion
3. Profound Perception
4. Enduring Charisma
5. Marksman At Arms
6. Cavalier By Cutlass
7. Invincibility At Sea

Knowing & understanding The Seven Elements of Captain Blue Eye could very well prove to be worth a full share of gold from the longest of adventures.

Ye May Be Diverse In Heritage & Unique In Manner, But Ye Must Be Vivaciously Aware Of The Importance Of The Captain's Crew.

— Captain Blue Eye

The Captain's Treasures

Types Of Treasures

The key to finding The Captain's Treasures is a combination of will, determination and information. Having one without the others will not provide the booty you seek, but if you have the will and determination, the information is available!

Information is obviously the most important part of your search and if you are viewing this web site, you may already have the will and determination.

Information on buried treasures come in a number of forms. Some information may be obvious such as on a treasure map, while other information may be not so obvious as within Tavern Journals, Ships Logs or other publications. Carefully analyzing every piece of information available for a specific treasure may save you valuable time.

For those with a desire for a quick dig and discovery, you may find your chest full of disappointment. Spending hours or days lifting every rock and walking around every tree is generally a waste of time. To be an efficient and effective treasure hunter, you must make educated decisions as to the specific location to begin your search. Nobody wants to spend a Saturday afternoon walking in the woods only revealing mosquito bites, thirst and hunger. Gather your information, be confident of the location, and then set out on your adventure.

Some educated searches for treasure may result in quick discovery (if you are the first pirate on location) while others may require more than one visit. Don't expect the treasure to be obvious as you walk by. A true treasure is hidden from the common visitor passing by and only revealed with the first successful treasure hunter.

One point to consider when searching for treasure is the treasure may not be buried in dirt or sand. The term "Buried" refers to the treasure being buried in mystery. The physical location of the treasure may be buried in dirt, sand, leaves or any other physical matter or the treasure may be hidden under, in or behind an object such as a tree, sign, building, rock, etc.

Treasure Coins

Captain Blue Eye's Treasure Coins are the most desired treasures buried by the notorious Pirate Captain. These Treasure Coins were designed by Captain Blue Eye himself! Each coin is made of precious metal and contains a unique engraving on each side. These Treasure Coins are part of Captain Blue Eye's Gold Reserve. Various Treasure Coins currently exist within The Captain's Gold Reserve. Of the many Pirate Gold Coins buried across the lands, three of the most sought after coins bring a reward of cash if properly returned to The Captain.

Some Treasure Coins come with a Certificate of Authenticity and has an independent serial number. The certificate is located within the treasure chest, along with the treasure coin. In order to claim your reward for these treasure coins, you must return the treasure coin to The Captain and report the appropriate serial number. Pirates returning Treasure Coins without reporting the associated serial number will not receive a reward. This is a security measure to prevent fraud and there are no exceptions!

The Rewards For Returning Treasure Coins To The Captain Are As Follows:

Gold Coins - 100,000 Pirate Gold or $1000 Dollars

Silver Coins - 50,000 Pirate Gold or $500 Dollars

Bronze Coins - 10,000 Pirate Gold or $100 Dollars

The Captain's Caches

Standard Cache Boxes

In addition to treasures, Captain Blue Eye has a number of cache boxes, which have been strategically placed throughout the lands. Cache boxes are utilized to assist crewmembers in their adventures. Cache boxes have been known to contain anything from information & supplies to pirate gold & cash.

At times, The Captain may use a specific cache box or a series of cache boxes to communicate with the crew. Various riddles & puzzles may appear unsolvable to the average sailor but an experienced pirate utilizing resources such as cache boxes may have the answers before the question is ever asked. Some locations may remain dormant for a period of time while others may be used quite frequently.

The location of a cache box may be discovered in a number of ways. Information may be passed or clues be given regarding cache boxes, but a well-equipped pirate needs no assistance from other pirates. In this modern age, the Captain uses improved techniques to locate cache boxes.

Utilizing modern technology and the capabilities of a GPS (Global Positioning System) the Captain has buried various Cache Boxes throughout the land. These Cache locations are unique and provide the well-equipped treasure hunter with a means to gather clues, maps and trinkets, which may eventually lead them to treasures.

Cache boxes should not be considered "Treasures". Treasures may contain various items of value, but not all cache boxes contain items of value. Cache boxes do, however, contain information within the logbook, which may become extremely valuable during various adventures.

When a pirate finds a Treasure, the entire Treasure is theirs to keep, even the chest. When a pirate finds a Cache box, the items within the Cache may be removed, but the Cache box should be left in the same location. Captain Blue Eye (or an associate) will eventually return to the Cache box to add additional items. If the Cache box is missing, no additional items will be left. In addition, the Cache location will be removed from the database and listed as a "Plundered Cache". No future Cache boxes will be placed at this location.

Once you discover a Cache location, you may want to revisit the location from time to time to retrieve any items recently placed. Each Cache location is restocked, but there is no "known" schedule.

Cache Cards have been known to contain information regarding specific Cache locations and some Treasure Maps have indicated several Cache locations within a specified area. Once you have discovered a Cache location, you may want to keep this information secret to increase your chances at retrieving the contents once restocked.

Visiting various cache locations and reviewing information within each logbook is highly recommended! At times, The Captain may summon a Captain's Call at a specific location. Details tend to be provided in various cache locations.

Series Cache Boxes

In addition to standard cache box locations, The Captain has a number of cache boxes grouped together in a "series". As with other cache locations, each cache box in a series is in a different location. The information alone, which is kept within each cache logbook in the series is quite valuable and may bring you fortune, if you know how to properly use it. There is an average of twelve cache boxes per series, with one notable exception.

The National Cache Series contains fifty cache boxes, with one cache box buried within each state. Pirate's fortunate enough to come across a cache box designated as part of the National Cache Series should immediately report the discovery to The Captain. Upon discovery of your first cache box within this series, The Captain shall reward your efforts and provide information to another cache box within this series. The first pirate to successfully discover and sign the logbook for each cache box within the National Cache Box Series shall be rewarded a prize worthy of a crown's smile.

To assist pirates in their adventure toward discovery of the National Cache Series, The Captain has provided coordinates to the first cache box within this series. The coordinates are as follows:

N38* 50.361   W105* 02.604

Once you have provided The Captain with proper information regarding your discovery of this cache box, additional information will be sent to you for your next adventure.

In addition to The National Cache Series of cache boxes, there are other "less challenging" cache box series providing notable rewards to successful pirates. Various regions contain one or two series of cache boxes while other areas contain many more. The southern region alone contains eight "known" series of cache boxes.

Due to the nature of the information contained within each series cache box, some are physically buried under sand, dirt or rock. If you track coordinates to a specific location, which appears to contain large amounts of sand, you may in fact be at the right location. Begin your search carefully, but take precautions to avoid being caught by other pirates.

All cache boxes, which are physically buried, must be reburied in the exact same location once you have plundered the contents and signed the log. If you fail to sign the log or take note of the information within during your visit, you may miss out on one or several unique opportunities!

If you discover a cache box during your travels and you are unsure of the possible association to a particular series of cache boxes, take a look on the inside of the front cover. If the cache box is associated with any series of cache boxes, the specific series will be noted here. In the southern region alone, there are currently ten "known" series of cache boxes currently discussed in local taverns

Ten "Known" Cache Box Series

1. The Golden Anchor
2. The Golden Barrel
3. The Golden Cannon
4. The Golden Cutlass
5. The Golden Flintlock

6. The Golden Key
7. The Golden Parrot
8. The Golden Sail
9. The Golden Spyglass
10. The Golden Tricorn

The Captain's Landmarks

Over the course of many adventures, Captain Blue Eye has mapped out each and every geographical area he has ventured through. With careful consideration to the many details of each area, as well as the known history of the location, Captain Blue Eye has given each location a specific name. Each name is unique and only provides reference to one specific location. The landmark name may be given based on a specific item, structure, point of interest, history of or person associated with the location.

As the Captain named each location in his travels, he took note of the common name used by the locals in the region. Some locations were known by various names while other locations were known by one or two names. In order to eliminate confusion in the future, the Captain noted his given name on a reference card along with the most common name used by the locals.

For example, Ponce Cove is known by the locals as Deleon Springs State Park. The Captain, therefore, has noted on a reference card that "Ponce Cove Be Known As Deleon Springs State Park".

Each Landmark Card provides reference to one specific location. Rumor has it there are a few rare publications that exist which provide a detailed list of all known landmark locations along with their common names. Some of these publications only provide landmark names for specific geographical areas while others are rumored to have a complete list of all named locations.

The Captain's Scuttlebutt

As noted in the Glossary, Scuttlebutt is defined as the latest rumor among the crew. Scuttlebutt has been known to both encourage and discourage individual pirates as well as entire crews on short and long adventures alike. Captain Blue Eye has taken measures to determine which scuttlebutt has merit and which has earned a descent to Davy Jones Locker.

For those rumors having merit and worthy of a pirate's ear, The Captain has noted the rumor on a Scuttlebutt Card. The Captain uses Scuttlebutt Cards to pass valid rumors along to loyal associates whenever there is a need for discrete communication.

At times, The Captain is not able to pass the scuttlebutt on to another pirate in person, therefore he tends to leave Scuttlebutt Cards in cache boxes or he'll place secret messages in Buried Treasure Bottles. Either way, scuttlebutt should be taken seriously and careful consideration should be given prior to passing along the latest scuttlebutt to another pirate.

Economy

Trade Goods

Trade Goods can be anything used in a successful trade with another pirate, merchant, tavern owner or other "persons of interest". In Pirates Buried Treasures, specific Trade Goods may be discovered, plundered, purchased or sold. These items may be used to barter for goods or services, or they may be sold for Pirate Gold or horded for a rainy day.

Commodities

Trade Goods listed as commodities have special requirements associated with their use, which a pirate must know and understand. When a Trade Good listed as a commodity, such as Wheat, Sugar, Coffee Grog & Rum, is applied to your account, the purchase/deposit date is noted in your profile. Commodities may not be traded or sold for one month after the item has been deposited. This one-month delay accounts for the travel time associated while sailing from port to port. This one-month period is for one calendar month, not a number of weeks or days.

For Example:

If a Trade Good is deposited on March 7th, you may not trade or sell this item until April 7th. There are no longer any exceptions for this one month delay.

Trade Goods listed as commodities vary in quantity & price, but rumor has it there are over fifty unique commodities in Pirates Buried Treasures.

The fifteen most common commodities, which tend to be found in Treasures, Caches, Buried Treasure Bottles, Taverns and many online locations such as houses & caves are as follows:

Common Commodities

Cedar	Grog	Silk
Chocolate	Oak	Sugar
Coffee	Pine	Tea
Cotton	Rum	Wheat
Flour	Salt	Wine

As the global economy expands into uncharted territory, the royal crown has increased its efforts of influence on merchants & trade routes. Regulation & taxation on trade goods from port to port has become an ever-increasing problem for those seeking profit. Supply and demand for various goods change with the tides, but the crown's increasing demand for an unfair share of each transaction has led even the most respected merchants to rely on smuggling certain trade goods for profit.

A well-informed merchant can earn a months salary with one transaction by utilizing the transportation services of a pirate, but with certain risks, there are consequences as well as rewards. If a merchant is caught employing the likes of a single pirate for any transaction with the intent of avoiding taxation from the crown, the merchant shall surrender all assets to the crown and be banished from future trade practices for a period of seven years. If the merchant is found to be in violation of the crowns order prior to the completion of the seventh year, the merchant shall be sent to the gallows.

Pirate Notes

In an effort to minimize liability and maximize opportunity, Captain Blue Eye has commissioned the use of special "Pirate Notes". Pirate Notes have been specifically designed to represent individual commodities and are used by pirates and merchants to conduct trade transactions without taxation by the royal crown. Pirate Notes, meticulously designed by The Captain, are currently in use within several trade groups and are quickly becoming the currency of choice.

As faith in local governments and the royal crown diminishes with time, pirates & merchants alike are requesting transactions to be made with Pirate Notes back by Captain Blue Eye. Pirate Notes are easy to smuggle from port to port and The Captain's reputation stands behind each note. The royal crown may not tax what they can't see and a vest full of Pirate Notes is easier to transport rather than a hold full of cargo. No other currency known to man bears the worthiness of a transaction like a Pirate Note from Captain Blue Eye.

Sample Pirate Notes

Artifacts & Idols

Artifacts & Idols are items found in both virtual and real world locations. These items vary in size and type as well as value. Each item contains an independent serial number and it's authenticity may be verified by e-mailing a request to The Captain or an associate. There is an unknown number of various Artifact & Idols in existence so you may want to acquire a Tavern Journal for more details.

Buried Treasure Bottles

Buried Treasure Bottles are small bottles, which contain one or several items buried in sand. Each type of bottle contains a different type of "Buried Treasure" and several bottles of the same type may contain various similar treasures with different values. Buried Treasure Bottles may be discovered or purchased, but it is recommended that purchases be limited to Taverns or other "official" PBT locations. Purchasing a Buried Treasure Bottle from another pirate brings the risk of paying for a bottle of sand, with no buried treasure within.

There are a number of Buried Treasure Bottles found within the world of Pirates Buried Treasures. Each type is identified by a unique symbol found on the label. The five most common Buried Treasure Bottles are as follows:

1. "Anchor" Buried Treasure Bottles
2. "Compass Rose" Buried Treasure Bottles
3. "Pirate" Buried Treasure Bottles
4. "Treasure" Buried Treasure Bottles
5. "Ship" Buried Treasure Bottles

The Captain's Cards

Pirate Profile Cards

Pirate Profile Cards provide pirates with an initial profile status, including login, password, rank, wealth (Pirate Gold) and equipment, if any. Profile status varies from card to card with some cards providing higher rank, better equipment and/or larger sums of gold.

Only one pirate profile may be used per pirate, but you may change profiles if you so desire. If you change your profile, your rank, wealth and items of value are automatically surrendered to the Captain. Your experience points, however, carries over to your new profile. Secondary profiles made be created under the same mailing address, but claims of discovery, scrolls & rewards will only be applied to one pirate profile.

Treasure Cards

Treasure Cards provide pirates with a unique opportunity to discover a specific treasure! Each pirate card comes with a treasure hunt name, card number, associated picture (usually of the treasure location) and a written clue regarding where the treasure is buried.

Cache Cards

Cache Cards provide pirates with GPS (Global Positioning System) coordinates to a specific cache box location. While some cache cards may only provide coordinates to the location of the cache box, other cache cards may provide a picture and a written clue as to the exact location of the cache. If a cache card provides a picture and written clue as well as GPS coordinates, the cache box is more than likely buried in sand, dirt or under a rock. The reason for this is quite simple...

When The Captain first began using cache boxes during his travels, a well-hidden location seemed to be appropriate for his needs & desires. Over time, various cache boxes were plundered or destroyed by rogue pirates, animals or natural disasters such as brush fires, floods and tornado's.

After careful consideration, The Captain began burying cache boxes to ensure the safety and integrity of the contents within. This method made some pirates frustrated during exploration, thus the need for additional information regarding "buried cache boxes". Finding a buried cache box tends to be more challenging, but the rewards within tend to greater as well.

Virtual Cache Cards

Virtual Cache Cards are similar to standard cache cards by having a set of GPS coordinates noted, but Virtual Cache Cards come with a twist. The Captain provides a set of coordinates to a specific location and also provides a question and a card number as well. If a pirate ventures to the location noted by the coordinates, they will be able to discover the answer to the question noted on the card.

Once the pirate has the correct answer to the question noted on the Virtual Cache Card, the pirate can email the answer and the card number to The Captain (or Quarterdeck). If the answer is correct, The Captain will provide the pirate with a reward.

Landmark Cards

Landmark Cards provide pirates with the name of a specific location The Captain has ventured to during his travels. The card also provides the "common name" for the location as used by the local natives. For those locations having more than one common named used by local natives, The Captain provides the most common name heard throughout his travels.

Scuttlebutt Cards

Scuttlebutt Cards provide pirates with the latest rumors having merit and worthy of a pirate's ear. Information noted on Scuttlebutt Cards should be taken seriously and careful consideration should be given prior to passing along this information to another pirate. Unlike most scuttlebutt passed from port to port, scuttlebutt noted on these cards tend to be of factual nature and have been confirmed by Captain Blue Eye.

Challenge Cards

Challenge Cards are unique cards that provide pirates with a challenge, question or task. Each Challenge Card comes with a question, challenge or task to complete, a card number and an associated value. If a pirate is issued a challenge card and either completes the challenge or task or has the correct answer, the pirate should send The Captain an email stating such information.

If the answer to the question noted on the card is correct or The Captain confirms the challenge or task has been completed, the successful pirate will receive the reward noted on the challenge card.

The level of difficulty of the questions, challenges and tasks associated with Challenge Cards vary and on occasion, may require a visit to a specific location. As with the level of difficulty, the reward amounts vary as well. The more difficult the reward, the larger the reward!

Other Cards

There are a number of additional cards found within the world of Pirates Buried Treasures, but these cards will be easily understood upon discovery. The Captain tends to leave cards behind during each and every adventure, so don't be surprised if one turns up near you!

Scrolls

As you journey through your pirate career, you may find yourself confident in your abilities and well armed with the knowledge and skills you have acquired through experience. For those seeking unique challenges, there are a number of Scrolls to test your confidence.

There are various types of scrolls available within Pirate's Buried Treasures, each with a unique challenge for the eager pirate armed with wits as sharp as a cutlass. The difficulty associated with each scroll varies as well as the information required to conquer each challenge.

Treasure Quest Scrolls

Treasure Quest Scrolls contain a series of questions, which must be answered completely and correctly to receive gold from The Captain. Some of the questions listed on Treasure Quest Scrolls may be about Pirates Buried Treasures while other questions may be about "other" pirate related things.

If you answer all of the questions listed on the Treasure Quest Scroll completely & correctly, you will receive 10,000 Gold ($100 Dollars) from The Captain.

Cache Quest Scrolls

Cache Quest Scrolls contain a single question, which must be answered completely and correctly to receive gold from The Captain. Cache Quest Scrolls only contain questions about Caches buried by Captain Blue Eye.

For seasoned pirates, Cache Quest Scrolls tend to be a reliable resource to fill your chests. For those pirates still searching for their sea legs, a Cache Quest Scroll may require an adventure to the Cache in question in order to solve the Scroll. If you answer the question noted on a Cache Quest Scroll completely and correctly, you will receive 5000 Gold ($50 Dollars) from The Captain.

Landmark Quest Scrolls

Landmark Quest Scrolls contain five questions regarding Captain Blue Eye's Landmarks. If you answer all five Landmark questions completely and correctly, you will receive 2500 Gold ($25 Dollars) from The Captain.

Riddle Scrolls

Riddle Scrolls tend to provide some of the most difficult challenges to pirates seeking adventures & treasures. Each Riddle Scroll provides a unique riddle, which must be solved completely and correctly in order to receive a prize from the Captain. The difficulties associated with Riddle Scrolls tend to vary, as well as the "Prize" for solving the riddle.

Adventure Scrolls

Adventure Scrolls tend to be the most difficult of all scrolls, but also provide the most valuable rewards. Adventure Scrolls are not to be taken lightly and are usually reserved for seasoned pirates. Those believing they may complete an Adventure Scroll in the comfort of their own home are sadly mistaken. They are called "Adventure Scrolls" for a reason!

Other Items Of Interest

As you set out on exciting adventures and explore the many opportunities available, you may come across a number of additional items worth their weight in gold! Information is the most valuable commodity known to man and there's plenty of it for those looking. Of the many forms of written information available, the three most popular forms are Treasure Maps, Tavern Journals and Ships Logs.

Ships Logs

Ship Logs are records of activity onboard a specific ship. Ship Logs may provide details on crewmembers, ship status, current or previous adventures or any other valuable pieces of information pertaining to the specific ship noted. The information alone usually brings the owner a significant price, but possession of a Ships Log usually provides rare and unique opportunities.

Tavern Journals

Tavern Journals are valuable items, which may provide a significant amount of information to those who may be in possession of one. Tavern Journals provide details of specific people, events or elements of Pirates Buried Treasures and usually answers a number of questions, which may otherwise be left unanswered. Each Tavern Journal is specific and only provides details on one subject.

A Tavern Journal may provide valuable information on a specific person such as a Tavern Owner or Barmaid or it may provide specific details on Trade Goods, Ships Logs, Artifacts, Idols or any other item of interest in the world of Pirates Buried Treasures. The acquisition of a Tavern Journal is rare indeed and should be exploited whenever the opportunity arises.

Treasure Maps

Treasure Maps are rare indeed, but none-the-less available throughout the world of Pirates Buried Treasures. Some treasure maps may be found in pieces, while others are still in tact. Pirates fortunate enough to come across a treasure map in whole or in part may find themselves well ahead of other pirates in pursuit of Pirate Gold.

A number of pirates have been known to find treasure maps in cache boxes, buried treasure bottles and tavern mugs as well as a number of online locations.

Online Adventures

Pirate Profiles

Your Pirate Profile is an essential element to your career as a successful pirate on the high seas of adventures & treasures. As discussed earlier, activating a pirate profile requires a Pirate Card. Once you have activated your pirate profile, you will use your profile page to manage your career as a pirate.

Pirate Profile pages contain all the information you need to manage your career as a pirate and is a helpful tool to use as reference when your mind is weary from travels or battles.

Pirate Profile pages contain everything from your service date, rank, wealth, attack & defense values, discoveries, personal challenge code, challenge record, personal effects on hand, inventory, "known" online locations with links, as well as various other helpful shards of information.

Personal Effects

Personal Effects are items, which may elevate your status as a successful pirate. Some items may provide you with additional advantages in future treasure hunts while others may provide you with "opportunities"! As you progress through your career, you will encounter various items, which you may purchase with your pirate gold. Your pirate profile page will contain details on items you have purchased and the effects will be seen as your various values change with new tools & equipment.

Many items classified as "personal effects" are items that may be worn, such as feathers, hats, gloves & boots or they may be carried such as daggers, swords, pistols & muskets. Each item you acquire may provide you with an advantage over other pirates during treasure hunts, captain's calls & pirate challenges.

The availability & price of each item classified as "personal effects" may vary from location to location and many items may be "discovered". Personal effects may be "found" in online locations such as taverns, houses & caves as well as Buried Treasure Bottles, Cache Boxes & Treasure Chests. If you discover and item either online or while out on an adventure, the item discovered will have a claim number.

Simply submit your claim number to the Quarterdeck and it will be applied to your pirate profile.

While on various journey's, you may encounter a number of scenarios where additional items may be extremely useful. There may be times when you may continue your adventure without having additional items on hand, but there will no doubt be times when you will have to analyze your inventory and possibly make another purchase or discovery before continuing. A well-prepared pirate tends to have a better chance of success over those lacking adequate supplies.

Pirate Challenges

Pirate Challenges are unique opportunities for a pirate to plunder another pirate for gold, personal effects and trade goods. In order for a pirate challenge to be initiated or accepted, you must first have your "challenge code". In order to keep seasoned pirates from preying on young and inexperienced sailors, challenge codes are only issued once a pirate reaches the rank of "Chum Master".

Once a pirate is issue a challenge code, they may challenge other pirates or be challenged themselves in a duel. Once a challenge has been initiated, The Captain handles the challenge and results are provided. Attack and defense values are calculated in a formula to determine the victor.

Once the winner has been determined, both pirates are notified and the winning pirate plunders all gold from the losing pirate. During decisive victories, the winning pirate may have an opportunity to plunder more than gold from his or her foe. More details regarding pirate challenges are provided to pirates once they are issued a pirate challenge code.

Online Locations

Within the world of Pirates Buried Treasures, you will no doubt discover unique locations and visit otherwise unknown locations from adventure to adventure. What many pirates don't know is there are a number of "online locations" to venture to as well!

The World Wide Web is filled with many locations unknown to most web surfers and is only known to pirates sailing the high seas with Captain Blue Eye. Of the many locations hidden in coves, havens & hideouts, Online Taverns seem to be the most popular of them all. Managed by old salts of the sea and assisted by fair maidens with plenty of rum, these taverns are open to any sailor with the knowledge of the correct address.

There be plenty of personal effects and trade goods available from tavern to tavern and no two taverns carry the same items. Scuttlebutt runs rampant and changes with the seasons and the most popular is usually posted near the head.

Of the many taverns hidden in the shadows, the seven most popular taverns (in no specific order) are as follows:

Popular Taverns
Dead Reef Tavern
Broken Hull Tavern
Seadog Tavern
Skull & Bones Tavern
Rumrunners Tavern
Rusty Anchor Tavern
Twisted Mast Tavern

There are a number of additional online locations such as houses, forts, dungeons, shipyards, caves & inns. Some may require a key to enter while others may be open to any weary traveler passing by. If you happen to discover an online location during your travels, send The Captain an email with the name and correct address. Upon verification of the correct address, a link will be added to your profile page for easy access.

Glossary

Abaft - Farther aft, as in "Abaft The Beam".

Abeam - On a relative bearing of 90 degrees (abeam to starboard) or 270 degrees (abeam to port)

Aboard - In or on a vessel

Abreast - Same as abeam

Admiral of the Black—Title of the leader of the Brethren of the Coast, an organization of buccaneers.

Adrift - Loose from moorings and out of control. Applied to anything that is lost, out of hand or left lying about.

Aft - Toward the stern. Not as specific as abaft.

After - That which is farthest aft, as after cannon.

Aground - When any part of the ship is resting on the ground (sand, shell, dirt, coral or rock). A ship runs aground or goes aground

"Ahoy, Matey"—Hail, fellow sailor.

Alee - In the direction toward which the wind is blowing (downwind).

All Fast - Tied or lashed down as necessary.

All Hands - The entire ship's company.

Aloft - Generally speaking, any area above the highest deck.

Alongside - By the side of the ship or pier.

American Main—Eastern coast of North America.

Amidships - An indefinite area midway between the bow and stern. Rudder amidships means the rudder is in line with the ships centerline.

Anchorage - An area designated to be used by ships for anchoring.

Armament - The weapons of a ship.

Ashore - On the beach or shore.

Astern - Directly behind the ship.

Athwart - Across or at right angles to.

Auxiliary - Extra or secondary,

Avast - Stop

Aye—Yes or any other affirmative reply.

Argh—The first word in any pirate's vocabulary. This word is used to punctuate any sentence and should be liberally sprinkled throughout the dialogue.

Barbary Coast—The Mediterranean coastline of North Africa, from Egypt to the Atlantic coastline.

Barnacles - Small shellfish that are found attached to the bottoms of vessels, pilings and other submerged objects.

Batten Down - The act of applying battens to a hatch.

Beam - The extreme breadth of a vessel or a frame supporting a deck.

Bear - The act of being located on a particular bearing, as in "the island bears 045 degrees".

Bear a hand - Provide assistance

Bearing - The direction of an object from an observer, measured in degrees clockwise from a reference point. True bearing is the angular difference between lines drawn from the observer to true north and to the object. Magnetic bearings the direction of the object measured on a magnetic compass. Relative bearing is the angle between the ship's head and the object.

Belay - To secure a line to a fixed point or to disregard a previous order.

Below - Downward, beneath or beyond something.

Berth - Bunk, Duty Assignment or mooring space assigned to a ship.

Bight - The middle part of a line or a loop in a line.

Bilge - Bottom of the hull near the keel.

Billet - Place or duty to which one is assigned.

Binnacle - Stand containing a magnetic compass.

Bitt - Cylindrical upright fixture to which mooring lines are secured aboard ship.

Bitter End - The free end of a line.

Black Jack—A leather tankard.

Block - A frame containing a pulley, called a sheave, around which a line (known as a fall) is rove.

"Blow the man down" – To kill someone.

Board - The act of going aboard a vessel.

Boat Boom - A spar rigged out from the side of an anchored or moored ship to which boats are tied when not in use.

Boatswain - Officer in charge of deck work (pronounced "bosun")

Boatswain's Chair - a seat attached to a gantline for hoisting a person aloft.

Boatswain's Locker - A compartment (usually forward) where line and other equipment used by deckhands are stowed.

Bollard - A strong, cylindrical upright fixture on a pier to which a ship's mooring lines are secured.

Boom - A spar, usually movable, used for hoisting loads.

Bow - The forward end of a ship.

Bow Hook - Member of a crew whose station is forward.

Break Out - To bring out supplies or equipment from a storage.

Breast Line - Mooring line that leads from the ship to the pier at right angles to the ship.

Brig - Naval term for jail.

Bring 'em Near—A telescope.

Bring 'er alongside"—Command to bring ships side to side for boarding.

Booty—Treasure.

Broad - Wide, as broad in the beam.

Broad on the Bow or Quarter - Halfway between dead ahead and abeam, and halfway between abeam and astern, respectively.

Broadside—All the guns on one side of a ship, also shots fired by that line of guns.

Buccaneer—Pirates who menaced the Spanish of the Caribbean.

Bulkhead - A wall onboard a ship.

Cackle Fruit—Hen's eggs.

Careen—To beach a ship and tip her on her side so the bottom can be cleaned and painted.

Cat O'Nine Tails—a nine thonged whip.

Chain Shot—Two cannonballs chained together and aimed high to destroy masts and rigging.

Corsair— Pirates of the Mediterranean.

Cutlass—A short heavy sword with a curved blade used by pirates and sailors.

Dance the hempen jig"—To hang.

Double Up - To double the mooring lines for extra strength.

Doubloons—Spanish coins found in pirate hoards.

Draft - The vertical distance from the keel to the waterline.

Drift - The speed at which a ship is pushed off course by wind and current.

"Emerald Shellback."—Sailor who has made the journey south of the equator and crossed at 00.00 Lat/00.00 Long.

Fake - The act of disposing of line by laying it out in long, flat bights, one along side the other.

fathom - Unit of depth equal to 6 feet.

"Feisty Wench"—Local Barmaid or other member of the female persuasion who chooses not to give in to a scurvy dogs demands.

Field Day - A day devoted to general cleaning, usually in preparation for an inspection.

Fire Ship — A ship loaded with powder and tar then set afire and set adrift against enemy ships to destroy them.

Flagstaff - Vertical staff at the stern to which the ensigns hoisted when moored or at anchor.

Fore & Aft - The entire length of a ship.

Forecastle - Forward section of the main deck. (pronounced fok-sul).

Foremast - First mast aft from the bow.

Forward - Toward the bow.

Foul - Entangled.

Gaff - A light spar set at an angle from the upper part of a mast. The ensign is usually flown from the gaff under way.

Galley - Space where food is prepared.

Gibbet Cage — Chains in which the corpses of pirates were hung and displayed in order to discourage piracy in others.

Gig - Small boat assigned to the captain.

Gold Road — Road across the Isthmus of Panama used to transport gold by train of pack mules.

Ground Tackle - Equipment used in anchoring or mooring with anchors.

Halyard - A light line used to hoist a flag or pennant.

Hand - a ship's crewmember.

Handsomely - Steadily and carefully, but not necessarily slowly.

"Hang 'im from the yardarm" — Pirate phrase for punishment for shipmates of captured prisoners.

"Hang the jib" — To pout or frown.

Hard Over - Condition of a rudder that has been turned to the maximum possible rudder angle.

"Head" — Location in the forward part of the ship used as a latrine.

Heading - The direction toward which the ship is pointing at any instant.

Heave - To throw

Heave-To — To come to a halt.

Helm - Wheel aboard ship used to turn the rudder.

Hempen Halter — The hangman's noose.

Hold - Large cargo storage area.

Hook - Familiar term for the anchor.

Hornswaggle — To cheat.

Hulk — British prison ships that captured pirates and privateers.

Hull Down - Refers to a ship that is so far over the horizon that only it's sails & mainmast are visible.

Inboard - Toward the centerline.

Inlet - A narrow strip of sea extending into the land.

Inshore - Close to the shore.

Jacob's Ladder - A portable rope ladder.

Jolly Roger — Flag declaring piracy, usually black with a white skull and crossbones or crossed swords.

Jump Ship - the act of deserting a ship.

Jury Rig - Any makeshift device or apparatus.

Keelhaul — A method of punishment aboard pirate ships in which the victim was tied to the ship, thrown overboard and dragged underwater along the length of the keel.

Knock Off - Quit working.

Knot - A method of forming an eye in a line or of tying the line to or around something. A term of speed which means nautical miles per hour.

Lanyard - Any short line used as a handle or as a means for operating some piece of equipment or a line used to attach an article to a peron.

Lash - To secure an object by turns of line.

Lay - Movement of a person as in "lay aloft".

Lee - An area sheltered from the wind. Downwind.

Letter of Marque—License by government to attack and loot enemy ships.

Lifeline - A line used to prevent a person from falling overboard or one used to recover a person that has already fallen.

Light Ship - The act of dispensing with blackout precautions.

Line - A term applied to a length of rope.

Log - A book or ledger in which data or events are recorded.

Look Alive - Admonishment meaning "be alert" or "move faster".

Lookout - Person stationed topside as a formal watch. This person reports all objects sighted and all sounds heard.

Lucky Bag - Locker under the charge of the Master At Arms and used to stow gear found adrift and deserter's effects.

Mainmast - Second mast aft from the bow.

Make Fast - To Secure.

Man - To assume a station.

Man-of-War—A vessel designed and outfitted for battle.

Marlinspike - Tapered steel tool used to open the strands of a line for splicing.

Marooned—To be stranded, particularly on a desert isle.

Mess - A meal. A place where meals are eaten.

Mate - A shipmate or another sailor.

Me—Used in place of "my".

"Measure ye fer yer chains"—To be outfitted for a gibbet cage.

Muster - A rollcall.

Nelson's Folly—Rum.

"No prey, no pay"—Crew received no wages, but shared in whatever loot was taken.

Overboard - Over the side of the ship.

Overhaul—To come up next to.

Overhead - The underside of a deck forms the overhead of the compartment below. It's never called a ceiling.

Pier - Structure extending from land out into the water to provide a mooring location for ships.

Pieces of Eight—Spanish coins found in pirate hoards.

Pipe - The act of sounding a particular call on the boatswain's pipe.

Pirate Round—Route from North America to the Indian Ocean.

Pitch - Vertical rise and fall of a ship's bow caused by head or following seas.

Plate Fleet—Fleet of Spanish ships used to carry silver and gold to Europe.

Pollywog - A lowly person who has never crossed the equator. Also known as "Wog".

Port - To the left of centerline when facing forward.

Privateers—Government sanctioned pirates, with permission in the form of a letter of marque.

Quarterdeck - Area designated as a place to carry out official business.

Quarters - Stations for shipboard operations.

Rat Guard - A hinged metal disk that can be secured to a mooring line to prevent rats from using the line to gain access to the ship.

Red Ensign—British flag.

Relief - A person assigned to assume the duties of another.

Riging - Lines that are used to support a ship's mast are called standing rigging; Those used to hoist or move equipment are called running rigging.

Ropeyarn - Term applied to an otherwise workday that has been granted as a holiday for the purpose of taking care of personal business.

"Run a rig"—To play a trick.

"Run a shot across the bow"—Command to fire a warning shot.

Sack - Bunk

Scallywag—A villainous or mischievous person.

"Scourge of the seven seas"—An extremely evil pirate.

Scurvy Dog—A prolific pirate.

Scuttle—To sink.

Scuttlebutt"—The latest rumor with the crew.

"Shellback"—Sailor who has made the journey south of the equator.

Shake A Leg - An admonishment to move faster.

Shake Down - The training of a new crew for developing efficiency in operating a ship.

Shift Colors - To change the arrangement of the colors upon getting underway or coming to moorings.

Shipshape - Neat & clean.

"Shiver me timbers"—phrase expressing surprise.

Sickbay - Shipboard space used as a hospital.

Six Pounders—Cannons.

Skylark - To engage in irresponsible horseplay.

Snub - The act of suddenly checking a line that is running out under a strain.

Spanish Main—Mainland taken by Spain, from Mexico to Peru plus the Caribbean islands.

Splice - The act of making an eye, or of joining lines together by intertwining strands.

Square Away - To put in proper order.

Square Knot - A simple knot used for bending two lines together or for bending a line to itself.

Stand By - To "prepare for" or "make ready to".

Starboard - To the right of the centerline as one faces forward.

Stay - Any piece of standing rigging providing support only.

Stem - Extreme forward line of bow.

Stern - The aftermost part of a vessel.

Stow - To store or pack items in a cargo space.

Swab - Same as, but never called, a mop.

Topside - General term referring to weather decks.

Trice Up - To secure bunks by hauling them up and hanging them off (securing them).

Turn In - To go to bed. Retire for the evening.

Turn Out - Get out of bed.

Turn To - Start Working.

Weather Deck - Any deck exposed to the elements.

"Wench"—Local Barmaid or other member of the female persuasion.

Whipping - Binding on the end of a line to prevent unraveling.

Windward - Toward the direction from which the wind is blowing.

"Wog" — *Lowest form of scum to sail the high seas. Wogs perform all dirty deeds onboard the ship until they prove themselves worthy of becoming an official member of the crew.*

Yardarm - *The port or starboard half of a spar set athwartships across the upper mast (a yard) is the port or starboard yardarm.*

Yaw - *The act of a vessel in having it's heading thrown wide of it's course as a result of a force from astern, such as a heavy following sea.*

Ye — *Used in place of "you".*

Captain Blue Eye is a legend living the dream and he enjoys each day as if it were his last. He urges those following to maintain a positive attitude through thick and thin and be thankful for yet another day in paradise. Gold, jewels and other material items may come and go, but treasured memories last a lifetime.

Of the many treasures hidden throughout life, time with your family is the most valuable treasure of all.

*With Every Adventure There Be Treasures To Plunder,
With Every Journey A Lesson To Learn.*

- Captain Blue Eye

The Black Flag Manual

YE BE WARNED!!!

No Pirate Shall Surrender Script To Friend Or Foe, Nor Shall One Be Inclined To Disclose Contents To The Royal Crown Or Local Governing Authority.

Violation Of Captain Blue Eye's Word
Shall Bring No Mercy!

© Captain Blue Eye
Pirates Buried Treasures
All Rights Reserved.

Notes From Adventures

Notes From Adventures

Notes From Adventures

Notes From Adventures

Notes From Adventures

Notes From Adventures

Notes From Adventures

Notes From Adventures

Notes From Adventures

Notes From Adventures

Notes From Adventures

Notes From Adventures

Notes From Adventures

Notes From Adventures

Notes From Adventures

Notes From Adventures

Notes From Adventures

Notes From Adventures

Notes From Adventures

Notes From Adventures

Notes From Adventures

www.ingramcontent.com/pod-product-compliance
Lightning Source LLC
Chambersburg PA
CBHW031224090426
42740CB00007B/696